SEA S

Consultant: Jerry Harasewych

Illustrators: Amy Bartlett Wright, Theophilus Britt Griswold

Copyright © 1999 National Geographic Society

Published by
The National Geographic Society
John M. Fahey, Jr., President and Chief Executive Officer
Gilbert M. Grosvenor, Chairman of the Board
Nina D. Hoffman, Senior Vice President
William R. Gray, Vice President and Director, Book Division

Staff for this Book
Barbara Brownell, Director of Continuities
Marianne R. Koszorus, Senior Art Director
Toni Eugene, Editor
Alexandra Littlehales, Art Director
Jennifer Emmett and Patricia F. Frakes, Writer-Researchers
Susan V. Kelly, Illustrations Editor
Sharon Kocsis Berry, Illustrations Assistant
Mark A. Caraluzzi, Director of Direct Response Marketing
Heidi Vincent, Product Manager
Vincent P. Ryan, Manufacturing Manager
Lewis R. Bassford, Production Project Manager

Visit our Web site at www.nationalgeographic.com

Library of Congress Catalog Card Number: 99-70467
ISBN: 0-7922-3458-8

Color separations by Quad Graphics, Martinsburg, West Virginia
Printed in Mexico by R.R. Donnelley & Sons Company

SEASHELLS

Jennifer Emmett and Patricia F. Frakes

Photographs supplied by Animals Animals/Earth Scenes
and Jerry Harasewych

NATIONAL
GEOGRAPHIC
SOCIETY

INTRODUCTION

Seashells come in an amazing variety of shapes, patterns, and colors. Most of the seashells that you find washed up on the shore are empty, but every shell once had an animal called a mollusk living inside. A mollusk is an animal with a soft body usually enclosed by a hard shell. A thin layer called the mantle covers the mollusk's body and produces its shell.

Four different groups of mollusks make the shells you are most likely to find on a beach. Chitons, a simple kind of mollusk, have an eight-piece hinged shell. The largest group of mollusks, gastropods, or snails, have a coiled shell with a single opening. Water enters one side of the opening, providing oxygen for the animal, and leaves the other side, removing wastes. Most snails have a hard attachment called an operculum that works like a trapdoor to block the opening of a gastropod's shell in times of danger. The third group of mollusks build shells shaped like an elephant's tusk. Tusk shells have openings at both ends. Bivalves, or clams, have a shell made of two valves that they can open and close.

HOW TO USE THIS BOOK

This guide covers some of the shells that you are most likely to find on the beaches and rocky shores of North America. Many are found in other parts of the world, too. The shells in this book are organized by the four main groups of mollusks that create them. First come chitons, then snails, tusk shells, and finally, bivalves. Each spread helps you identify a kind of shell and tells you about it. A shaded map shows where the shell is found in North America, and the "Field Notes" entry gives interesting facts about its size and color. If you see a word you do not know, look it up in the Glossary on page 76.

LOOKING AT SEASHELLS

It's easy to lose track of time when you're out looking for shells, so be sure you're wearing protective clothing—a T-shirt and hat—and sunscreen to avoid sunburn. Beaches can be made of sand or rocks. If the shore is rocky, wear rubber-soled shoes to protect your feet.

Each day ocean waves roll into shore and then roll out again. At high tide the waves reach the highest point on a beach. At low tide the waves reach the lowest point. Hollows in rocks that hold water as the tide goes out are called tide pools. The part of a beach between the high tide line and the low tide line is called the intertidal zone. The best time to go shelling is right after a storm or at low tide, when retreating waves leave a lot of new shells in the intertidal zone.

Bring containers for the shells and a shovel to dig them up. A magnifying glass helps study the details of a shell. Use a sieve to strain sand to find tiny shells.

A mollusk's shell is never shed while the animal is alive. If you find a snail with its operculum blocking the opening, or a clam that is tightly closed, the mollusk inside is alive. Put the shell back where you found it. Make sure it is legal to take shells from the beach you are visiting.

When you take your shells home, wash and scrub them with an old toothbrush. If they still smell, ask an adult to help you soak them in a mixture of one part bleach and nine parts water. Rinse them, then let them dry in the sun.

Keep a field notebook of where you find your shells. Note the beach and the location, the season of the year, the time of day, and the date you found each shell.

CHITON

 A chiton (KI-tuhn) is a very simple mollusk. It has no eyes. The shell of a chiton is made of eight overlapping plates surrounded by a muscular band called a girdle.

WHERE TO FIND:
Look for chitons on or under rocks or stones and in tide pools along both coasts of the United States.

WHAT TO LOOK FOR:

✳ SIZE
Most chitons range from less than one inch to three inches long.

✳ COLOR
They can be green, brown, black, yellow, white, or pale orange.

✳ BEHAVIOR
A chiton attaches itself to a home base, where it stays during the day.

✳ MORE
At night a chiton creeps out to dine on algae. It returns to its base at dawn.

Muscle-like strips between the plates of its shell allow a chiton to bend. It curls up into a ball when it is disturbed.

FIELD NOTES

The chiton got its nickname, coat of mail, because its plates look like the suit of armor that knights wore.

LIMPET

A limpet attaches itself to a rock with a foot that works like a suction cup. The bond a limpet creates is so strong that it led to a saying: A person who hangs on to someone else "clings like a limpet."

FIELD NOTES

A limpet spends a large part of its life waiting for the tide to come in so that it can eat and breathe.

The ridges of a limpet shell channel splashing water off its surface. This helps counteract the intense force of waves.

Look for limpets in the intertidal zone of rocky shores from Arctic seas to warm waters of the tropics.

WHAT TO LOOK FOR:

✳ SIZE
Most limpets are ½ to 1 inch long.

✳ COLOR
A limpet can be white, orange, gray or brown. Some limpets have rays of color.

✳ BEHAVIOR
Limpets usually live clustered together in large colonies.

✳ MORE
A limpet scrapes algae and seaweed off rocks with many rows of file-like teeth.

ABALONE

Abalones are bases for many other animals. Seventy kinds of tiny mollusks have been found living on one red abalone. Abalones are a favorite food of sea otters.

WHERE TO FIND:
Abalones live on rocks below the high tide line along the Pacific coast of North America.

WHAT TO LOOK FOR:

✳ **SIZE**
An abalone can be 4 to 12 inches long.

✳ **COLOR**
Abalones are generally red, green, or black on the outside.

✳ **BEHAVIOR**
Like all mollusks, abalones get oxygen from the water. It flows in under the shell and out through holes in the top.

✳ **MORE**
Abalones are also known as "ear shells" because of their shape.

Apache Indians considered abalone shells so sacred that they made ceremonial jewelry from them.

Light bouncing off the layers of an abalone shell makes the shiny interior look pearly or blue-green.

13

TOP SHELL

The shape of a top shell can tell you where it spent its life. If a top shell has lived in calm, sheltered water, it may have a high pointed top. Top shells in areas with rough seas usually are less pointed.

A top shell takes about six years to reach its adult size.

14

0000000000
FIELD NOTES
Top shells got the
name because
their high, pointed
shape makes
them look like
children's toys.

WHERE TO FIND:
You'll find top shells in the intertidal zone of temperate and tropical areas of the continent.

WHAT TO LOOK FOR:

❋ SIZE
They range in size from as small as your fingernail to as long as your hand.

❋ COLOR
They may be white, gray, brown, or black. The inside of the shell is shiny.

❋ BEHAVIOR
Top shell snails move along rocks or other surfaces looking for plants to eat.

❋ MORE
Top shells may be covered with seaweed, which can make them hard to find.

NERITE

Gastropod (snail)

There are more than a dozen different kinds of nerites in North America. Nerites live in saltwater and freshwater. They are found on rocky shores and in rivers and swamps.

WHERE TO FIND:
There are huge numbers of saltwater nerites along all the tropical coasts of North America.

WHAT TO LOOK FOR:

* SIZE
The largest nerite is about two inches long.

* COLOR
They come in many colors and patterns.

* BEHAVIOR
Nerites live in large colonies.

* MORE
Nerites eat only plants. Some nerites store water in their shells to keep from drying out at low tide.

Like these emerald nerites, all nerite shells are thick and round and have an opening shaped like a half circle.

CERITH

GASTROPOD (SNAIL)

 Like most snails that burrow in mud or sand, ceriths have long, narrow shells. Ceriths live in large colonies on sheltered beaches and in bays, marshes, and swamps.

WHERE TO FIND:
Ceriths live in sandy areas in shallow waters from Alaska through southern North America.

WHAT TO LOOK FOR:

✳ SIZE
Most ceriths are about two inches long, smaller than the length of your first finger.

✳ COLOR
Ceriths may be white, brown, black, or speckled.

✳ BEHAVIOR
They lay their eggs in long, jelly-like strands that look like thin spaghetti.

✳ MORE
They feed on bits of plants and animals.

Look for ceriths below the high tide line on a beach. Some crawl around on the surface. Others dig down into the sand in search of food.

FIELD NOTES
Often, the best way to find ceriths buried on a beach is to sift the sand through a coarse sieve or strainer.

PERIWINKLE

Periwinkles survive out of water because they can store it inside their shells. Their dull colors help hide periwinkles and make them hard for predators to find.

FIELD NOTES

A periwinkle leaves a slimy path as it moves. The slime allows the snail to glide along a rocky surface.

Like most snails, the periwinkle adds to its shell as it grows. Each addition, or complete turn of the shell, is a whorl (WORL).

WHAT TO LOOK FOR:

✳ SIZE
Periwinkles range from ⅛ inch to 1¾ inches long.

✳ COLOR
Most periwinkles are white, gray, or brown. Some are yellow or orange.

✳ BEHAVIOR
They often swarm on rocks or seawalls.

✳ MORE
Different kinds of periwinkles may live on the same rocky shore, each kind at a different distance from the waterline.

CONCH

 A conch shell is easy to spot on a tropical beach because of its size and its brightly colored outer edge. Once this edge is formed and spreads outward, a conch stops growing.

WHERE TO FIND:
Conchs live among sea grasses in sandy shallows from the southern coast of the U.S. into the tropics.

WHAT TO LOOK FOR:

* SIZE
Conchs can grow to be as long as a cereal box turned onto its side.

* COLOR
They are usually pale with a pink or deep-colored interior.

* BEHAVIOR
A conch moves by anchoring its foot in the sand and pulling its shell forward.

* MORE
If the tide throws a conch ashore on its back, it uses its foot to turn itself over.

Queen conchs, like this one, have been known to produce pink pearls.

SLIPPER SHELL

A slipper snail spends its life attached to a rock, another shell, a horseshoe crab, or even a piece of sea grass. Slipper snails that settle on sea grass grow long, narrow shells.

Slipper snails often live stacked on top of each other. The smallest and youngest are at the top. The oldest and largest are at the bottom.

24

A shelf over part of the opening of this shiny shell makes it look like a tiny satin bedroom slipper.

WHERE TO FIND:
These shells are common on sandy beaches, in warm and cold seas, throughout North America.

WHAT TO LOOK FOR:

✳ SIZE
Slipper shells range from the size of your thumbnail to two inches in length.

✳ COLOR
They are cream, dark brown, reddish purple, and sometimes spotted.

✳ BEHAVIOR
The very young mollusks, called larvae, drift for months before settling.

✳ MORE
This snail creates the shelf in its shell to protect the softest parts of its body.

CARRIER SHELL

This shell can look like a mound of broken shells or a pile of rocks. To help it hide from its enemies, a carrier snail adds rocks, shells, and other hard objects to its shell as it grows.

Some carrier shells have been found with pieces of glass, bottle tops, and other trash attached.

WHERE TO FIND:
Carrier shells live in warm waters, often in sandy areas, from the U.S. through the Caribbean.

WHAT TO LOOK FOR:

✳ SIZE
They are two to three inches across. With covering, they may seem larger.

✳ COLOR
From above, none of the original shell of a carrier is visible.

✳ BEHAVIOR
These snails attach whatever is near so they will blend with the background.

✳ MORE
They have been around for millions of years. They are the first shell collectors!

FIELD NOTES
Without its covering of camouflage, the carrier shell is thin and has a wide opening.

WORM SHELL

A worm snail grows in a spiral. The shell looks as if it had a real worm inside. This mollusk starts life as a tightly coiled snail. It forms a long extended tube only after it attaches itself to a rock or a sponge.

FIELD NOTES

Worm snails live in clusters and must curl out to find food. These shells are also called old maid's curls.

WHAT TO LOOK FOR:

❋ SIZE
Worm shells can grow to be two to six inches in length.

❋ COLOR
They can be white, brown, or orange.

❋ BEHAVIOR
Once these snails attach themselves, they will never move again.

❋ MORE
They wave threads of sticky mucus through the water to catch tiny plants and animals to eat.

If you look closely at the small end of this worm shell, you can see the tight coil where the snail began forming it.

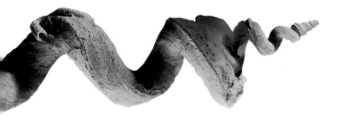

COWRIE

These "jewels of the sea" have glossy, china-like shells. They look as if they have been polished by hand, but the smooth, shiny surface is natural.

Cowries were once used as money in many areas of the world, including China and some parts of Africa.

WHERE TO FIND:
Although cowries exist all over the world, only five kinds are found in North American waters.

WHAT TO LOOK FOR:

✳ SIZE
Cowries range from less than an inch in length to longer than an adult's hand.

✳ COLOR
Cowries may be gray, pale yellow, brown, speckled, banded, or spotted.

✳ BEHAVIOR
When it is crawling, a cowrie's mantle almost completely covers the shell.

✳ MORE
When disturbed, a cowrie pulls back its mantle to expose its shiny shell.

FIELD NOTES
Since the time of early man, cowries have decorated religious objects such as this African mask.

MOON SHELL

GASTROPOD (SNAIL)

A moon snail inflates its foot with seawater until it is much larger than the shell and almost covers it. Moon snails also use the large foot to burrow into the sand in search of clams to eat.

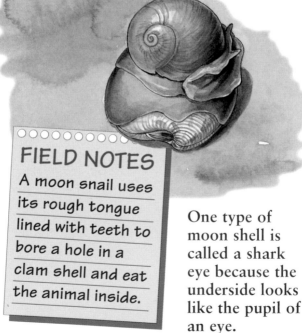

FIELD NOTES
A moon snail uses its rough tongue lined with teeth to bore a hole in a clam shell and eat the animal inside.

One type of moon shell is called a shark eye because the underside looks like the pupil of an eye.

WHAT TO LOOK FOR:

✳ SIZE
They measure ½ to 5 inches across.

✳ COLOR
They are dark brown, reddish brown, or white.

✳ BEHAVIOR
Moon snails protect their eggs in collar-shaped cases they make with fine sand.

✳ MORE
A moon snail may eat three or four small clams a day.

HELMET SHELL

Helmet snails feed on spiny sea urchins, sand dollars, and sometimes even dead crabs. Two tentacles used for touching help the helmet snail find food. Its eyes are located at the base of the tentacles.

Knobby and heavy helmet shells are sometimes cast ashore by waves and found almost buried in sand.

WHERE TO FIND:
Look for helmet shells in shallow waters from the eastern United States through the Caribbean.

WHAT TO LOOK FOR:

✳ SIZE
Helmet shells are 4 to 14 inches long.

✳ COLOR
They are white, brown, orange, and black and come in various patterns.

✳ BEHAVIOR
One kind of helmet snail lays its eggs in the shape of a tall, round tower.

✳ MORE
Since ancient times helmet shells have been used to make lamps, scoops, and cups.

FIELD NOTES
The dark and light layers of a helmet shell offer artists an ideal material for carving delicate cameos.

TRITON'S TRUMPET

GASTROPOD (SNAIL)

 The Triton's trumpet is named after Triton, a god of the sea in ancient Greek myth. All over the world, people of different cultures have used Triton shells as horns.

WHERE TO FIND:

Tritons are found mostly in shallow waters near coral reefs from southern Florida to the Caribbean.

WHAT TO LOOK FOR:

✳ SIZE
A triton can be as long as a ruler.

✳ COLOR
The shells are cream colored, with dark brown blotches or curvy lines.

✳ BEHAVIOR
Tritons secrete a poison that numbs their prey. They feed on other mollusks.

✳ MORE
Triton shell horns have been found in cave dwellings from the Stone Age.

White teeth with brown between them ring the opening of a Triton's thick shell.

FIELD NOTES

In Greek myth Triton blew his shell trumpet to calm the wild seas and rivers after a violent storm.

WENTLETRAP

GASTROPOD (SNAIL)

 The wentletrap's name comes from the Dutch for "winding staircase." Wentletraps have a ribbed and pointed shape with bulging turns, or whorls.

WHERE TO FIND:
Wentletraps live in all seas, from shallow to deep water. Look for them in tide pools and along beaches.

WHAT TO LOOK FOR:

✳ SIZE
They range from a ¼ to 1 inch long.

✳ COLOR
Almost all are white or whitish.

✳ BEHAVIOR
Some wentletraps secrete a poisonous fluid that they use to numb prey.

✳ MORE
One species, the precious wentletrap, was a rare collectors' prize in the 17th century. Today it is more common.

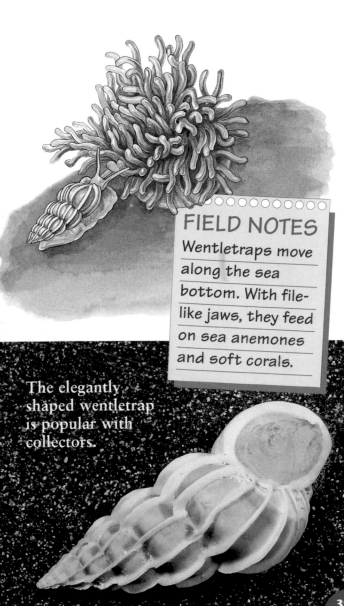

The elegantly shaped wentletrap is popular with collectors.

JANTHINA

 Janthinas, also known as purple snails, feed on the Portuguese man-of-war, a kind of jellyfish. These snails drift in ocean currents.

WHERE TO FIND:
Janthinas live in warm water in the open sea. They are found along both coasts of North America.

WHAT TO LOOK FOR:

✳ SIZE
They can grow to two inches in length.

✳ COLOR
Janthinas usually have a light blue top and a deep purple bottom.

✳ BEHAVIOR
Floating upside down, janthinas fool predators such as fish and birds by blending with the sky and the sea.

✳ MORE
In addition to eating jellyfish, they sometimes feed on each other.

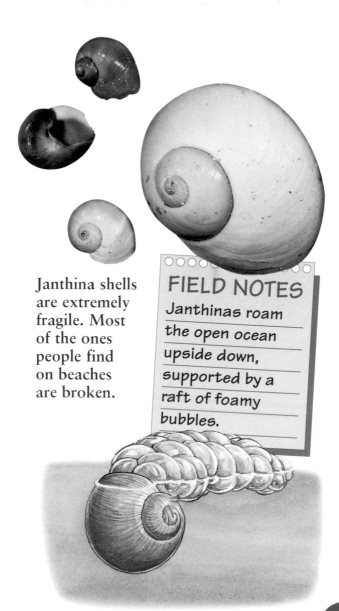

Janthina shells are extremely fragile. Most of the ones people find on beaches are broken.

FIELD NOTES

Janthinas roam the open ocean upside down, supported by a raft of foamy bubbles.

WHELK

There are many kinds of whelks. They are found in seas of all temperatures. The female snail lays egg capsules. When the eggs hatch, larvae crawl or swim away.

WHERE TO FIND:
Whelks are found on sandy beaches and in bays throughout North America. Some live in deep water.

WHAT TO LOOK FOR:

✳ SIZE
Some grow to finger size; others reach the size of a hand—or larger!

✳ COLOR
Large whelks are usually white or gray.

✳ BEHAVIOR
Whelks are often caught in baited traps.

✳ MORE
Whelks are meat eaters, or carnivores. They eat oysters and other bivalves. Whelks also feed on dead animals, among them fish and crabs.

Northern whelks are generally drab in color and design, while tropical whelks have more shades and patterns.

Sailors used some types of whelk egg capsules to clean their hands. They called them sea wash balls.

MUREX

 Whether frilly, spiky, spiny, or smooth, murexes are among the most unusually shaped shells in the sea. Some murexes on reefs look like the coral that surrounds them.

WHERE TO FIND:
Most murexes live in tide pools and on rocks and coral reefs throughout North America.

WHAT TO LOOK FOR:

✳ SIZE
Murexes can be large shells, up to ten inches long; most are one to two inches.

✳ COLOR
They are white, gray, or brown—known for their shapes, not their coloring.

✳ BEHAVIOR
They use a special tooth to drill holes in the shells of animals such as clams.

✳ MORE
Drilling can take from a few hours to a few days—a long wait for a meal!

FIELD NOTES

Phoenicians crushed murex shells to produce a rare purple dye used in cloth worn by royalty.

Some murexes, like this one, live in water deeper than 1,000 feet. Others live in shallower water and are more likely to wash up on the beach.

OLIVE SHELL

Olive shells are known for their distinctive, often tent-like patterns and polished surfaces. They live in sand—sometimes in colonies that number into the thousands.

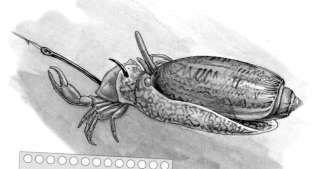

FIELD NOTES

Olive snails are attracted to fishing bait and may be caught on fishermen's hooks or in baited traps.

The tent olive has a pattern of interlocking triangles that looks a little bit like a snowy mountain range.

Olive shells are found in sandy areas of most temperate and tropical seas from Alaska south.

WHAT TO LOOK FOR:

✳ SIZE

Small olives, called olivellas, are the size of a grain of rice; other olives grow to five inches in length.

✳ COLOR

Olive shells come in many patterns and colors, but are often brown and white.

✳ BEHAVIOR

They burrow in sand to eat small snails.

✳ MORE

Native Americans wore olive shells as jewelry.

CONE SHELL

Cone shells are some of the most attractive in the sea, but they are also among the deadliest. Cones inject poison to subdue their prey—usually worms, other snails, or fish—before eating it.

FIELD NOTES

Some cones spear fish with a special hollow tooth, inject poison, then swallow their prey whole.

Their beautiful and distinctive patterns make cone shells collectors' items. Rare species are quite valuable.

WHERE TO FIND:
Cones are found in all tropical and subtropical seas. They live on rocks, coral reefs, or in sand.

WHAT TO LOOK FOR:

✳ SIZE
Cones range from the size of a peanut to more than 8½ inches in length.

✳ COLOR
Cones come in all colors. They usually have vivid and elaborate patterns.

✳ BEHAVIOR
Some tropical Pacific cone shells are poisonous enough to kill humans.

✳ MORE
All live cones should be handled with great care.

AUGER SHELL

Augers prey mostly on marine worms—and swallow them whole. Bigger animals prey on the auger. A crab uses its claws to break an auger's shell and eat the animal inside.

WHERE TO FIND:
Augers are often found in small colonies. They live in shallow water in temperate and tropical seas.

WHAT TO LOOK FOR:

✳ SIZE
Most are less than 2 inches long, but a few may reach 8 or 10 inches.

✳ COLOR
Augers range from white to red to brown and often have spots or stripes.

✳ BEHAVIOR
Certain types of augers live where waves crash onto the land and drift along shore with the currents.

✳ MORE
Some augers hide under rocks or coral.

All augers are long and slender and taper to a sharp point. The opening is at the broad end of an auger shell.

FIELD NOTES

This cross section reveals the interior spiral pattern of an auger. All snails build their shells in coils.

VAMPIRE SHELL

GASTROPOD (SNAIL)

 Vampire snails feed on the blood or body fluid of their prey, usually without killing it. Most feed on soft-bodied animals that live on the sea bottom.

WHERE TO FIND:
Look for vampires below the low tide line throughout North America. Some live in depths of 5,000 feet.

WHAT TO LOOK FOR:

✳ SIZE
Vampire shells range from fingernail size to 3¼ inches in length.

✳ COLOR
They are mostly white, brown, or tan, often with bands of color.

✳ BEHAVIOR
Some vampire snails feed on clams.

✳ MORE
One vampire snail has an open coiled shell. The whorls do not touch each other. The shell looks like a corkscrew.

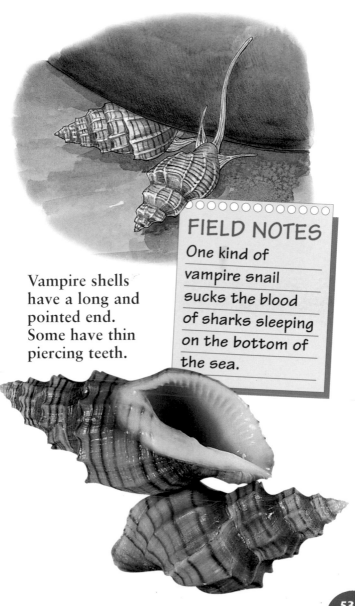

Vampire shells have a long and pointed end. Some have thin piercing teeth.

FIELD NOTES

One kind of vampire snail sucks the blood of sharks sleeping on the bottom of the sea.

SUNDIAL SHELL

 Sundials get their name from their shape. They look much like sundials, circular instruments that use the sun to tell time. These shells grow in an even, curving spiral.

WHERE TO FIND:
Sundials live buried upside down in sea grass beds in warm waters. They come out at night to feed.

WHAT TO LOOK FOR:

✳ **SIZE**
Sundial shells may reach 1½ inches in width.

✳ **COLOR**
They are usually whitish to tan, with dark brown bands, spots, and speckles.

✳ **BEHAVIOR**
Many sundials eat the tender tissue of soft corals or other still sea creatures.

✳ **MORE**
Larvae begin coiling their shells one way, then switch direction as adults.

Sundial surfaces are marked by many spiral bands and small, delicate bead-like bumps.

FIELD NOTES

From the underside of a sundial, its center point, or umbilicus, is visible. The shell coils around this point.

BUBBLE SHELL

GASTROPOD (SNAIL)

Bubble snails have small, thin shells and large bodies that are sometimes red or yellow. Bubble snails are close relatives of a group of snails that have no shell at all—the sea slugs.

FIELD NOTES

Most bubble shells are so fragile that they offer the animal little protection against enemies.

Bubble shells are often clear and very delicate in appearance. Some are even called paper bubbles.

Usually bubble shells live in sandy or muddy areas, from shallow waters to great depths.

WHAT TO LOOK FOR:

✳ SIZE
Bubbles are small shells, usually less than an inch in length.

✳ COLOR
Most are white or nearly transparent. Some are brown with stripes of color.

✳ BEHAVIOR
Bubble shells lay their eggs in long, jelly-like strands.

✳ MORE
Most are carnivores that swallow prey whole. Others eat only algae.

TUSK SHELL

Tusk shells look different from the shells of chitons, gastropods, and bivalves. A tusk shell is shaped like an elephant's tusk. It is long, thin, and slightly curved. Tusk shells are open at both ends.

FIELD NOTES
In the Pacific Northwest, Native Americans used tusk shells as wampum, or a kind of currency.

The tusk takes water in through the narrow end. It brings in food and releases waste through the wide end.

WHERE TO FIND:
Tusks live in shallow to deep water buried in sand or mud. Their narrow end stays just above the surface.

WHAT TO LOOK FOR:

✳ SIZE
Tusk shells grow as long as three inches, but most are less than one inch.

✳ COLOR
Whitish or gray in color, some tusks are smooth, while others have ribs.

✳ BEHAVIOR
Tusks find their food, a type of single-celled animal, in the sand.

✳ MORE
Hermit crabs sometimes use empty tusk shells as their homes.

MUSSEL

A mussel is a bivalve, a type of mollusk also known as a clam. A bivalve shell is made of two matching halves, or valves, joined by a hinge. These halves open and close.

WHERE TO FIND:
Mussels often live in cold-water areas, in tide pools, on rock piers, between high and low tide lines.

WHAT TO LOOK FOR:

✳ SIZE
Most mussels are between one and three inches long.

✳ COLOR
The common blue mussel is dark blue. Others range from black to green.

✳ BEHAVIOR
Mussels anchor themselves to hard surfaces with thin, hair-like threads.

✳ MORE
Mussels survive outside the water by holding their breath.

Mussels are often found mixed with other shells. Look for them in piles of shells washed up on the shore.

Mussels live in dense colonies on places such as rocks or pilings, sharing space with other animals.

OYSTER

 Many oysters have grooved lines in their top shells. These lines are growth rings. The mantle, a soft, fleshy part of the oyster, adds to the shell, layer by layer, causing the rings.

WHERE TO FIND:
Oysters of many kinds live in temperate to tropical seas, generally anchored to rocks, reefs, or other oysters.

WHAT TO LOOK FOR:

* SIZE
Most are about three inches long.
Some grow to more than six inches.

* COLOR
Oysters are grayish white.

* BEHAVIOR
They sometimes grow on top of each other, forming large oyster bars or reefs.

* MORE
Oysters are usually oval, but they can grow into less regular shapes when crowded by their neighbors.

Oysters have a rough outer shell, usually covered by mud, and a white interior.

SCALLOP

Scallops, unlike most bivalves, can swim. That's exactly what they do to escape predators such as sea stars. Some scallops use thin, hair-like strands to anchor themselves to hard surfaces, as mussels do.

WHERE TO FIND:

Scallops live in warm and cold waters. Some attach to rocks or piers. Others live in sandy places.

WHAT TO LOOK FOR:

✳ SIZE
They range from ¼ to about 6 inches across. Rarely, they reach 11 inches.

✳ COLOR
They come in an array of delicate and brilliant colors from white to crimson.

✳ BEHAVIOR
By rapidly opening and closing their shells, scallops swim in zigzags.

✳ MORE
The scallop has a double row of tiny, brilliant blue eyes.

FIELD NOTES
The elegant and balanced shape of the scallop has frequently inspired decorations in art and architecture.

The Lion's Paw scallop has bulges. Most other scallops have only ribs or are smooth.

THORNY OYSTER

 Thorny oysters are not oysters at all. They are more closely related to scallops. The spines characteristic of this shell can grow quite long in deep, gentle waters.

WHERE TO FIND:
Most thorny oysters live in fairly deep water, usually in the tropics. They often live among coral.

WHAT TO LOOK FOR:

✷ SIZE
They range from one inch to six inches in length. Some grow even larger.

✷ COLOR
Thorny oysters come in many, often bright colors, including a fiery orange.

✷ BEHAVIOR
They attach themselves permanently to a hard surface such as rock or coral.

✷ MORE
Divers often find thorny oysters when exploring shipwrecks.

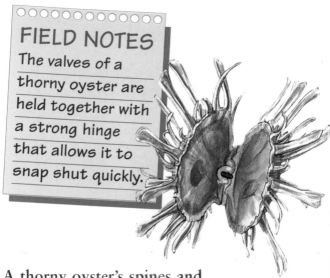

The valves of a thorny oyster are held together with a strong hinge that allows it to snap shut quickly.

A thorny oyster's spines and bright colors are often hidden by algae and sponges that cover it.

COCKLE

 Cockles are also called heart clams because they look like hearts when closed and viewed from the side. Some cockles are ribbed, some smooth, and others prickly.

WHERE TO FIND:
Cockles live in warm waters near the surface in sandy and muddy areas, but they stay buried.

WHAT TO LOOK FOR:

✳ **SIZE**
Egg-shaped or rounded, cockles can be less than one inch or more than five inches in diameter.

✳ **COLOR**
Colorful shells, they range from yellow, pink, and orange, to brown or white.

✳ **BEHAVIOR**
Cockles are active clams and can jump several inches using a powerful foot.

✳ **MORE**
Many fish eat cockles.

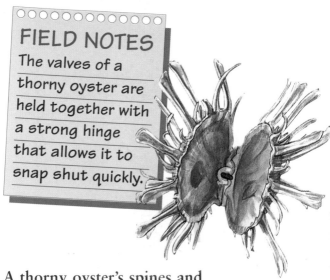

A thorny oyster's spines and
bright colors are often hidden by
algae and sponges that cover it.

COCKLE

 Cockles are also called heart clams because they look like hearts when closed and viewed from the side. Some cockles are ribbed, some smooth, and others prickly.

WHERE TO FIND:
Cockles live in warm waters near the surface in sandy and muddy areas, but they stay buried.

WHAT TO LOOK FOR:

✳ SIZE
Egg-shaped or rounded, cockles can be less than one inch or more than five inches in diameter.

✳ COLOR
Colorful shells, they range from yellow, pink, and orange, to brown or white.

✳ BEHAVIOR
Cockles are active clams and can jump several inches using a powerful foot.

✳ MORE
Many fish eat cockles.

Deep grooves distinguish this brown-speckled cockle. Cockles are related to giant clams.

69

COQUINA

BIVALVE (CLAM)

 Coquinas are often found in huge numbers on sandy beaches. They may be washed about by the surf. Some are solid pastel colors, and some have stripes.

WHERE TO FIND:
Look for coquinas on almost any sandy beach in either temperate or tropical regions.

WHAT TO LOOK FOR:

✳ SIZE
Coquinas are very small, only about ¼ to less than 1 inch long.

✳ COLOR
Coquinas come in an array of pastels.

✳ BEHAVIOR
The animal has a pair of tubes, called siphons, one to bring water into the body and one to let it out.

✳ MORE
Some coquinas wash up and down the beach with rising and falling tides.

Coquinas are also called butterfly shells for their wing-like appearance.

ANGEL WING

BIVALVE (CLAM)

 Angel wings have beautifully shaped shells with delicate ribs and notches. This clam uses the blunt end of its shell to burrow up to three feet deep in mud or sand.

WHERE TO FIND:
Angel wings live in deep burrows they dig along the shores of tropical and temperate seas.

WHAT TO LOOK FOR:

✳ **SIZE**
An angel wing can grow to more than 8 inches in length.

✳ **COLOR**
Angel wings are white to grayish white and may be tinged with pink.

✳ **BEHAVIOR**
They may spurt water as they burrow.

✳ **MORE**
The shell of an angel wing is very fragile and is easily broken if the animal leaves its burrow.

FIELD NOTES

The foot of the angel wing clam is contained by its shell, but its long siphons extend beyond it.

The beautiful shape of open angel wings shows how they came by their common name.

SHIPWORM

A shipworm is a clam with a very long, worm-like body and a tiny shell at one end. These clams use their sharp shells to bore into wood, where they live.

WHERE TO FIND:
Shipworms live in all seas where wood is found. They are common in North America south of Canada.

WHAT TO LOOK FOR:

✳ **SIZE**
The shell of a shipworm is ⅛ to ⅜ inches wide. The mollusk may grow up to 2 feet long.

✳ **COLOR**
These shells are white or whitish.

✳ **BEHAVIOR**
Some shipworms coat their burrows with a hard white material they make.

✳ **MORE**
The burrows of shipworms, rather than their tiny shells, become their homes.

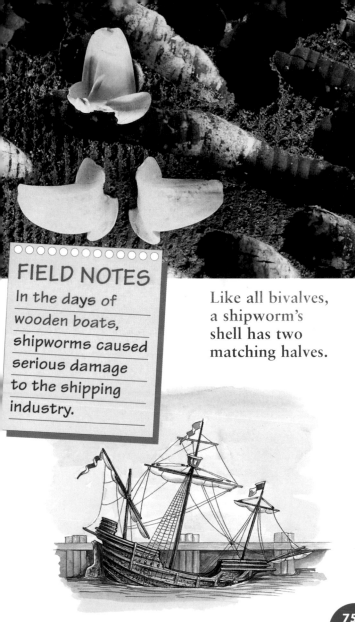

In the days of wooden boats, shipworms caused serious damage to the shipping industry.

Like all bivalves, a shipworm's shell has two matching halves.

GLOSSARY

bivalve A type of mollusk (also called a clam) with a shell composed of two matching halves, or valves, connected by a hinge.

chiton A type of mollusk with an eight-piece interlocking shell.

gastropod A type of mollusk (also called a snail) with a shell that is a single coiled tube.

larva A name for a very young mollusk just after it hatches from its egg. A larva looks very different from an adult.

mantle A thin layer that covers the internal organs of a mollusk's body and produces its shell.

mollusk A type of animal with a soft body surrounded by a mantle. It usually has a shell.

operculum A type of trapdoor that seals the opening of a mollusk's shell.

predator An animal that hunts and kills other animals for food.

siphon A tube that mollusks use to take in or expel water.

temperate Not extreme. Temperate seas are those in the northern and southern portions of the globe. Waters may be warm or cool depending on the season.

tropical Characteristic of the tropics. Tropical seas are warm year-round.

tropics The region lying north and south of the Equator that is warm all year-round.

tusk shell A type of mollusk that has a long, curved, tapering shell with an opening at each end.

umbilicus The central cavity around which a snail's shell is coiled.

whorl One complete coil of a snail's shell.

INDEX OF
SEASHELLS

ABOUT THE CONSULTANT

Dr. Jerry Harasewych first became interested in seashells at the age of six. He now uses submarines to study and collect mollusks and their shells in the deep sea. He is the Curator of Marine Mollusks at the National Museum of Natural History, Smithsonian Institution, editor emeritus of *The Nautilus,* and a member of the board of the Bailey-Matthews Shell Museum in Sanibel, Florida.

PHOTOGRAPHIC CREDITS

Photographs supplied by Animals Animals/Earth Scenes and Jerry Harasewych

front cover Jerry Harasewych **back cover** Victor R. Boswell Jr., NGP **half title page** Fred Whitehead **title page** Victor R. Boswell Jr. NGP 5 Paul A. Zahl, NGP 9 Richard Shiell 11 Zig Leszczynski 13 Patti Murray 14 E.R. Degginger 17 Patti Murray 19 Jerry Harasewych 21 Jerry Harasewych 23 G.I. Bernard 24 Patti Murray 26 (both) Jerry Harasewych 28-29 Victor R. Boswell Jr., NGP 30 Zig Leszczynski 33 Zig Leszczynski 34 Peter Weimann 37 Jerry Harasewych 39 Patti Murray 41 Patti Murray 43 Fred Whitehead 45 Victor R. Boswell Jr., NGP 47 Richard Kolar 49 Jerry Harasewych 51 Patti Murray 53 Jerry Harasewych 55 Jerry Harasewych 57 Jerry Harasewych 59 Patti Murray 61 Michael Gadomski 63 Breck P. Kent 65 Jerry Harasewych 67 Joyce & Frank Burek 69 Fred Whitehead 71 Carson Baldwin, Jr. 73 Jerry Harasewych 75 Jerry Harasewych 77 Victor R. Boswell Jr., NGP 79 Fred Whitehead